The Journey

The

A Tale of Hope

Mark E. Hundley

"To Run is to Pray!" Hopi Proverb

The Journey *is a work of fiction. With the exception of some references to the author's own personal experiences related to the death of his first wife as well as his early childhood, all names, places, and incidents either are products of the author's imagination or are used fictitiously. Where appropriate, the author has worked to weave into this story, his own personal experiences with loss and grief.*

All rights reserved. No part of this publication may be reproduced, distributed, or transmitted in any form or by any means, including photocopying, recording, or other electronic or mechanical methods, without the prior written permission of the publisher, except in the case of brief quotations embodied in critical reviews and certain other noncommercial uses permitted by copyright law. For permission requests, write to the publisher.

Copyright © 2018 Mark E. Hundley, M.Ed., LPC

Dedication

I dedicate this story to the courageous children and families served by the **Journey of Hope Grief Support Center** in Plano, TX and to all children everywhere who lose a loved one to death. No other life experience invades and affects the lives of young people more than the death of a loved one. To all charged with navigating life without your loved one, may your **Journey** be filled with **Hope** and **Healing**! To all who dare to serve as companions in this process, may your experience be one of Grace and Love.

May you find and share Peace!

Mark E. Hundley

The Journey

A puddle . . . That's all it was! Just a puddle in the middle of the sidewalk. Little did I know that striding into that dark patch of liquid in the pre-dawn hours of a typical Saturday morning would alter my life so much – so completely! I still wonder at times whether I dreamt the entire experience or . . . Well, let me explain.

Running is something I have done most of my life. As a young child running was part of my play, a natural extension of my curiosity about the world around me. With each year added to my lifespan, running evolved into a kind of companion for me, an alter ego of sorts. In grade school, I quite inadvertently discovered that running could add status and stature as well. Up until the time I participated in my first "footrace," running had just been . . . running.

That first race on the playground in Plainview, TX, opened a new world for me. When the teacher dropped her hand for all first grade boys to race from the starting line drawn on the playground dirt to where she was standing, I reached the finish line comfortably ahead of the "competition." I recall the euphoria as my friends clamored around me exclaiming how very fast I was!

"Me? Fast?" I really hadn't given it any thought before. That day ushered in years of running – on the football field; on the baseball diamond; on the basketball court; on the track and on the street. I loved running because I was good at it! I was in charge of ME! It wasn't so bad for my ego either. Coaches loved my speed; my parents marveled at my skill; my friends wanted to hang with me because of it; and, well, the girls loved it too! I felt just plain special. Over the years, I collected ribbons, medals, trophies and ink to certify that I was one running dude!

Don't go looking in the record books for my name, because you won't find it! As with any physical gift, personal exclusivity of possession does not exist. There are always others gifted in the same way who are just a little faster, just a little better and my days of domination quickly faded in high school.

Privately, away and apart from the hoopla, running provided a sense of wholeness at a spiritual level that escaped comprehension or articulation as a child and teen. I just knew that I felt good about life and myself when I ran. Not until years later in adulthood when life became more complicated did I grasp the power afforded me by the ability to run.

The Journey

~~~~~~~

Eventually, jogging replaced sprints; spikes gave way to "running shoes;" 5K and 10K t-shirts substituted for medals and ribbons; personal accomplishment supplanted public accolades. I ran all the way through college in the years when jogging was earning its "legs" as an acceptable form of exercise. I ran all the way through 12.5 years of marriage – for health; for recreation; for stress relief. I ran for those reasons until the day I couldn't for just *those* reasons anymore. I ran until the day running meant living.

January 24, 1989, changed MANY things in my life, the least of which was my running regimen. New Year's Day 1989, my wife Christy and I had committed to running the White Rock Marathon together the following December! We had even begun training. That late January morning changed everything! A mere two hours after Christy left our house for work, I found myself in an emergency waiting room hearing unfathomable words from a physician – Christy was . . . dead!

The injuries inflicted on her body in a car accident earlier that morning were inconsistent with her survival. I suddenly found myself as the single father of a seven year-old daughter – desperate; bewildered; numb! What would I do? I had no idea. Following the blur of activity surrounding her funeral and the immediate aftermath, I found myself floundering. I had to do something to cope!

One thing I DID do that literally saved my life, was run! I discovered that regardless of the weather – rain, snow, or heat – I could run and cry and no one would know whether tears or sweat or moisture streamed down my cheeks (not that casual observers riding in vehicles paid any attention to a crying jogger). I trained for and ran two marathons over the next two years raising money for a memorial scholarship. I ran for health. I ran for therapy. I ran for sanity.

Several years later, I worked with some dedicated individuals to create a non-profit organization that focused on providing grief support for children and the **Journey of Hope Grief Support Center** came into existence. What did I do beyond the creation of the center? Well . . . I ran! I ran to raise awareness and funds for this precious organization. With each step in each race, people responded by giving to the cause! The excitement and sense of accomplishment drove me to continue – until it didn't anymore. Until I began hearing from my body that 5:00 am was just too early; that multiple miles per week were damaging my joints (by the way, my feet and legs told me this and I've since learned to question their "truthfulness"); that there are always others out there able to take my place and do what I do.

Frankly, I wanted to listen. I was looking for a reason, ANY reason to scale back or quit altogether. I almost did too, until my encounter with that danged old puddle.

The Journey

~~~~~~~

As I stepped out on the porch for my pre-run stretch that Saturday morning, a full moon hovered overhead while stars flashed indecipherable messages in an HD clear cobalt sky. The mid-40's temperature chilled my limbs causing goose bumps to explode all over my exposed skin. I shivered, half tempted to return to the warmth of my bed. Refusing to give in, however, I instead turned up the volume on the mp3 player allowing Brooks and Dunn's ***That's What It's All About*** to jump-start my sluggish engine. Looking back, I guess I should have considered that the words to that song foreshadowed something unexpected on the path before me, but hindsight *is* always 20/20. I took off for yet another run in the still, early morning hours.

Rounding the corner and heading down the familiar sidewalk along side the street, the moonlight and corner street light seemed to suddenly battle for the direction in which to send my silhouette. In a crossfire of conflicted shadow casting, my silhouette seemed to both move forward and backward at the same time. Fascinated by this playful optical illusion, I could have sworn that the part of my shadow that lurched ahead actually freed itself from the invisible moorings around my feet and sprinted away in the distance.

"Must be seeing things," I remember saying to myself as I continued to run down hill. Still, a twinge of uncertainty nipped at the heels of my imagination. Had something or *someone* actually run ahead of me? "Nah, just mind tricks!" Still . . .

I continued to run, allowing the words of the song to take my mind off the strangely unsettling visual anomaly just encountered. Ahead of me in the middle of the sidewalk lay a familiar site – a puddle. I was used to puddles on this route since the sprinklers often left them as calling cards, reminding of the dutiful fulfillment of their appointed task of ensuring the continuation of the landscape. Harkening back to my childhood, I had a choice about how to approach the obstacle in front of me. I could run around; jump over; or just plow through hoping to dodge the chilled splatter droplets as I did so! At that particular moment, I decided to plow right on through, thank you!

What happened next was well . . . just plain weird! As I prepared to plant my foot in the middle of the puddle, words from the song seemed to send everything into slow motion. B & D were singing *"It's a moment frozen there in time when the reasons all begin to rhyme . . ."* (McEwan & Wiseman) and my foot came down on what should have been water with solid concrete underneath. Instead, I found myself sinking into and through the dark liquid. I clutched in vain at the sidewalk as it disappeared above my head. I tumbled into nothingness. The song continued – *"where love's a little bigger and you finally start figuring out. That's what it's all about!"* (McEwan & Wiseman)

I braced myself for the inevitable crash of body to ground, but instead seemed to float slowly downward as if buoyed by a parachute. After a few moments, my feet gently touched down on a solid surface. As I landed, the music abruptly ceased, the once brilliant moonlight disappeared into darkness and deafening silence engulfed me.

I sat down not wanting to make things worse than they already were. Nothing made sense. I didn't know where I was. Ultimately, I decided that I must have slipped in the water, hit my head and was in la la land. Surely, my mind would clear soon and I could be on my way. "Man, am I going back to bed as soon as I can get up from here," I remember saying. If only it had been that simple.

As I sat still, I reached for the back of my head expecting to encounter a sore, protruding goose-egg created by my foolish attempt to go through the puddle; however, my fingers found no bump whatsoever. Things were getting stranger by the second!

I recall thinking that I must surely have landed flat on my back and therefore, covered by water from the puddle. Nope! Dry as a bone. I had no idea what was going on, then it hit me! I was dreaming! That's what it was – a dream! I breathed a sigh of relief. Now I could just enjoy this twisted experience knowing that I would wake up soon. I sat still and closed my eyes.

"You ok?" The voice in front of me broke my silent reverie.

"What? Oh, yeah, I'm fine. Just wiped out in my dream. That's all," I responded with eyes still closed thinking that a new character had been added to my flight of fancy.

My new companion spoke again. "Well, I just wanted to make sure you arrived safely – no sprained ankle or broken bones or anything like that."

"Broken bones," I chuckled to myself! Now *that* would take the cake! Breaking a bone in a dream!

As if my yet unseen companion read my mind, he responded, "Oh, *this* is no *dream*, my friend. You are very much awake and this place is very real!

I suddenly felt exposed and vulnerable – a little scared too! Where in the heck was I? What had happened?

"Go ahead," my companion spoke again. "Open your eyes.

The Journey

You have miles to run before you sleep again."

However, I didn't want to open my eyes. In addition, I *certainly* didn't want to think about running – what – *miles* he had said? I just wanted to continue to believe that I was dreaming.

"We don't have much time," he spoke again. "Please open your eyes."

As I reluctantly responded, I noticed that pre-dawn light had filtered into the area in which I was sitting, casting a grayish lavender hue, slowly nudging the suffocating darkness away.

"Here, let me help you up! You've gotta get going!"

For the first time, I looked up into the face of my companion – only there wasn't really a "face" so to speak. Perhaps he was still in the shadows because his silhouette was all that I could make out. I reached up to grasp his outstretched hand. Although I felt the warmth of skin on skin, it was as if I were taking the hand of a shadow – a substantive shadow, mind you, but a shadow nonetheless.

As I stood beside my companion, I noticed that he was dressed in the same manner as I – running shoes, shorts, sleeveless shirt and cap. He could have been a carbon copy of me. Whoa! What a thought! Shadow! Carbon copy! The entire scene from a few moments earlier came roaring back creating even more confusion. I froze!

Once again, my companion appeared to read my mind. "We are similar, you and I. We share the same passion for helping people – the same dedication to making a difference. Don't worry. I am not a figment of your imagination! I am real and will be your coach on your journey through this **Place of Passage**. I want to help you answer the questions that have been dogging you lately."

Well, you could have knocked me over with a feather! I was completely undone! Before I could form the words of questions spinning through my brain, a kind of "understanding" infiltrated my thinking and I knew – I just *knew* that this **Place of Passage** was a "place between places" – a place visited often but rarely recognized – a place of answers; a place of questions; a place of discovery; a place of purpose. I also knew that I had appointments to keep. I didn't know how. I just knew.

I turned to look into the face of my "coach" only to have my breath taken away. Although his form still blended with the shadows, his eyes seemed to capture and reflect the miniature explosions of light set off by all the stars in the Universe. When he smiled back at my amazement, it was if the essence of the blue-white full moon projected from his face into the lavender mist in front of me revealing an archway with a wooden gate separating me from space on the other side. Etched into the top of the archway were words that beckoned me forward.

My companion said, "Read on and follow the instructions."

As I gazed up at the inscription, the reason for my presence in that place became crystal-clear.

"Since you are surrounded by such a great cloud of witnesses, put aside all that weighs you down and entangles you and run with endurance the race that is set before you . . . keeping

your eye on the finish line. Strengthen your arms and knees. Make level paths for your feet so that others will be healed by your efforts." (Hebrews 12:1-3, 12 paraphrased)

"You have far to go and much to learn," Coach said. "Are you ready?"

"Looks like I don't have much choice," I responded feeling a bit put upon.

"You know, you asked for this journey – this is of your own making," He said. "Your serious deliberations about the purpose of your running caused you to come to this place."

Having quickly learned that the weird was common occurrence in that place, I decided not to quibble. He was right – I guess. I *had* created the opportunity for personal exploration – although maybe not in the manner it took place. Clarifying the purpose of my running at *this* stage of my life was more important than perhaps anything I had done in quite some time – and I was *ready* – at least I hoped I was.

The Journey

As I moved toward the gate, Coach touched my shoulder and I stopped. He said, "Here. You'll need this in order to navigate what lies ahead."

With that, he opened the palm of my right hand and placed a small oblong, slightly teardrop shaped disc, then gently closed my fingers around it. As he did so, the gate opened before me.

"I'll see you down the road," he said as I walked through and began instinctively jogging down the misty path.

The Journey

～～～～～

    Still working to wrap my mind around my walk on the weird side, the air around me suddenly filled with almost palpable electricity. I half-way expected to feel lightning course through me with the next step. Instead, a humming sound assaulted my ears – a sound much like that of a thousand active beehives. It grew in intensity with each step. Seeking the source of the noise, I slowed a bit and an amazing sound transition occurred. With the decreasing speed of each step, the once indecipherable humming became more familiar – like voices all speaking at once. I caught bits and pieces of words spoken by yet invisible people that seemed to emanate from every direction in the mist – words tinged with emotion and urgency; some even desperate and pleading in nature. Finally, I ceased running altogether.

    As I slowed to a stop, the source of the sounds abruptly materialized! There in the mist, hundreds, perhaps *thousands* of people stood, stationed alongside the path on which I was jogging. They stood in a vast stadium towering above the path at 45-degree angles on both sides, extending upward beyond my line of sight. I would likely have remained motionless forever; however, my enchantment with the scene vanished when I realized that all gazes and therefore all *words* projected in my direction. I felt ill at ease and wanted to disappear into the ground. Then, the words from the inscription began to sink in – *"surrounded by such a great cloud of witnesses"* – and things began to fall in place. These folks were here to cheer me on – to offer encouragement on my journey! "How cool," I thought! I started running again and the intensity of their cheers immediately increased. I was pumped! I was ready to take on the world!

The Journey

~~~~~~~

The cheers gradually faded as I moved forward and found myself striding down an isolated and unfamiliar path through what appeared to be a park of some sort. The tangerine tinged clouds overhead told me that full sunrise was imminent. As I approached a clearing, an overwhelming sense of fear, panic and uncertainty gripped me. I slowed down so that I could determine the source of those feelings. From out of the shadows created by a copse of trees, I saw perhaps twenty or so people emerge, making their way toward the path on which I ran. I say people because they looked rather ethereal in nature; ghostlike. I could almost see through them as they moved in unison. What captured my attention most was the look on their faces. Agony etched every feature.

I felt trapped! Not knowing what would happen next, I sprinted forward in an effort to escape my own fears as much as those who approached me – to no avail. An older woman moved with uncanny speed and planted herself squarely in front of me. The others vanished. I screeched to a halt to avoid running into her. She reached out and gently touched my cheek. My vision spun wildly as she spoke. "Please! I need your help."

A type of mental connection between the two of us ensued. Without words, Belle (the name of the grandmother who stopped me) allowed me to see what had happened to her. It seems that Belle was the sole caregiver for her two grandchildren ages 8 and 10. Their mother, Belle's daughter, was a drug addict who had abandoned the children on Belle's doorstep when they were just one and three – abandoned them and disappeared. No one knew the identity of the biological father so Belle – widowed herself ten years earlier – had adopted the kids and was raising them on her own. She was doing a wonderful job too until the day she suffered a heart attack and died while they were in school.

Understandably, Belle was worried about their future – their well-being. The children were now wards of the state and would soon become part of the foster care system. That worry accounted for the sense of agony experienced earlier. The more I "listened" to her story, the more I realized that those feelings channeled from the children through Belle to me. When that realization sank in, my heart shuddered with pain. I remember looking into Belle's clear blue eyes asking, "What do you want *me* to do?"

For the first time in our encounter, she spoke directly to me. "I need you to tell their story. I need you to do everything you can to let the authorities know that those two require special care – especially in dealing with my death. I was all they had! I was it!"

As I pondered the gravity of this situation, she spoke again.

"I need you to do this not just for them, but for all the other children who find themselves in similar circumstances. The people given charge of orphans need to know how to help children mourn so that they can heal properly and grow to be healthy adults! Please!"

I remember feeling helpless and impotent as I responded to her. "I . . . I'll do my best, Belle. I don't know how, but I will do the best I can," I said. "I'll do the best I can."

Belle reached out and squeezed my shoulder. "I know you will, son. I know you will." Her smile penetrated the cloak of helplessness that draped my heart and I felt somewhat optimistic. I began to believe that I *could* do something after all.

"Now run along," she said. "You have many more miles ahead of you." With that, she walked back into the shadows smiling back at me over her shoulder as she disappeared.

The Journey

Shaking off the haze created by the encounter, I turned and jogged down the path, around a corner and emerged through a thin veil of fog into a heavily wooded area. To my surprise, ice and a light dusting of snow covered the woods. A narrow, winding path snaked through the tall trees before me. Although I should have been cold, I was completely unaffected.

I continued to run, enjoying the scenic beauty. After a few minutes, I topped a small hill and saw something at the base of one of the trees up ahead. As I approached, I was compelled to investigate. Nailed on one rather large tree was an intricately woven metal cross. I stopped and knelt before the tree and noticed that a small rock lay on the ground just below the cross. I brushed the snow from the smooth face of the rock and discovered that it bore and inscription. It said, "***In loving memory of Brian.***" Just above the inscribed stone, the tree revealed a deep gouge – a scar that had permanently damaged its rugged surface.

Feelings of extreme sadness and concern overwhelmed me. I focused on the words, which led me to wonder who Brian was and what had happened to cause someone to create such a touching memorial. So engrossed by the feelings associated with this loving memorial, I was almost unaware that a slight breeze stirred the limbs of the tree in front of me. Not until the tinkling sound of a wind chime hanging on a branch above wrested my attention from the memorial did I realize that I was not alone. I looked to the right of the tree and saw someone standing there dressed in blue jeans and sneakers. Startled by the presence of another person, I rose abruptly and stared into the face of a young man, perhaps 18 or so years of age. He nodded to me. I was immediately aware of the identity of this young man.

"Hello, Brian," I said.

Brian said not a word, but reached out and placed his hand on my shoulder. His touch transported me into the backseat of a car in which Brian was a passenger, riding "shotgun" in front. Neither Brian nor the driver were aware of my presence. I observed both Brian and his companion being teenagers – typical young men out for a drive. The gist of the conversation revealed that they were on their way back to a friend's house following an outing to the local burger joint. A fine powder of light snow covered the winter roads. The speed of the car approached a dangerous level for such conditions. Distracted by conversations, they did not notice. I was powerless to do anything about the situation.

Suddenly, the tires spun out on a slick patch of ice concealed by the snow and the car began whirling wildly. Once, twice, three times the car careened between the street curbs. Without warning, the vehicle jumped the curb nearest the median and slammed into a tree on the passenger side – Brian's side – of the car! Although I was impervious to the physical impact, my spirit strained against my body in an attempte to escape.

Then, I knew what had happened to Brian. The inevitability of the ensuing crash had caused me to close my eyes. Brian gently squeezed my shoulder and I opened them once again. He wanted me to see more.

What came next were visions of a series of visitations to that tree by many, many people – friends, acquaintances and . . . family. I watched as the memorial evolved into what lay at the foot of the tree at which we stood. Four years had come and gone since the accident had inalterably changed the lives of so many. My heart ached for each person who participated in countless pilgrimages to that memorial. I wanted to somehow ease the pain – tell them that things could eventually get better.

I looked into the hazel eyes of a young man so very full of promise – so intent on making a difference in this world. There before me stood a young man released from this life far sooner than intended – a young man who had a message for *me*.

"What do you want me to do, Brian?" I asked sincerely. "What do you want me to do?"

Simply stated he said, "Help them believe!"

"Believe? Believe what, Brian? And who? Who am I to help? I don't understand," I responded.

"Please help my family to believe in themselves – in each other. Help them hold on to the parts of their faith that actually make sense – those things that give meaning to life. Help them believe in their abilities to negotiate the obstacles ahead of them. Help them believe that they have the power to navigate through uncharted waters and heal. Help them believe that life is more than just the things that are tangible. Help them believe so they can help others believe as well."

I knew the meaning of his words. When the unthinkable had happened in my life, all my beliefs exploded into the air. I struggled to nail down those beliefs that truly helped *me* go through life altered by loss.

Once again, I realized that the feelings of sadness and concern were actually coming from Brian's family. They were working hard to reconcile themselves to the tragedy and create meaning through their mourning. His parents carried heavy hearts, both for Brian's loss as well as the pain experienced by his brothers and friends.

"Help them believe," he said. "Help them believe!"

I ducked my head and responded, "I'll do my best, Brian. I'll do my best."

With that, Brian released my shoulder. When I looked up, he was gone. Although I had no idea where to begin, I had made a promise. I would find a way.

The slight breeze once again stirred the wind chime to life and I smiled at the courage and character Brian left behind in our encounter. I would carry those with me on the remainder of my journey.

I resumed my trek through the woods on the winding path, lost in contemplation. Topping a hill, I found myself on a rather steep downward slope filled with loose rocks. I slowed in order to maneuver the trail. Ahead of me was a tree laden with a very thick blanket of snow that threatened to fall and block my path. About the time I reached the branch, the snow blanket released and I found myself diving through the cascade. I barely made it through untouched. When I rolled to a stop, I looked up and found myself on a service road next to a busy interstate highway in *New Mexico*!

The Journey

~~~~~~~

This was a familiar stretch of I-40 west of Santa Rosa where the Sangre de Cristo Mountains slightly north and west of my location begin talking shape. Becoming more familiar with the protocol of this weird excursion, I dutifully began jogging, looking around for the next person I would encounter. Cars and trucks whizzed by in both directions on I-40 just beyond the fence. Although the sun was at its pinnacle, the temperature was most comfortable, making for an enjoyable jog. A sudden gust of wind kicked up dust and bits of dry prairie grass causing me to stop and shield my eyes. As I wiped the tiny particles from my face, extreme anxiety swirled around in my chest squeezing air out of my lungs. I struggled to breathe deeply and felt as if I were in a full-blown panic attack. I felt as if I would faint when . . .

I felt a woman gently take my hand in hers. Immediately, the invisible constriction released and my breathing returned to normal. I opened my eyes and found myself face-to-face with a very attractive young woman about 32 years of age. Instinctively, I knew that her name was Angela. I worked to prepare myself for *her* story. As quickly as the wind had whipped sand and grass into action only a moment ago, her story played out in holographic form.

It seems that mere months ago – eleven to be exact – Angela went in for her yearly exam and discovered rapidly growing uterine cancer. The news of her illness took her entire family by surprise; yet, the aggressive nature of the cancer was even more shocking. Despite all efforts from the best doctors available, Angela

The Journey

succumbed to the ravages of this terrible disease, leaving behind a boy age 9 and a girl age 7 as well as her wonderful husband of 12 years – Malcolm. Her story – *his* story – paralleled mine so much that I retreated into my own tortured memories until she squeezed my hand once again bringing me back to that moment.

The confusion I felt must have been evident because her eyes told me that I would soon understand the purpose of this stop. Her gaze moved out toward the Interstate and mine followed. Somehow, she directed my focus to a single car speeding west toward Albuquerque. As I looked on, I realized that her family occupied the vehicle. As this realization took hold, I found myself immediately transported to the front passenger seat of the car. As before, I sat undetected.

Malcolm appeared wound tighter than a drum – clinging so desperately to the steering wheel that his knuckles bulged white through his skin. His countenance projected unchecked anxiety and panic. His heart pounded, sounding as if horses raced through his chest cavity. His breathing was as rapid as if he had just participated in a 100-meter sprint. I got the distinct impression that he was on the run; that he was intent on getting away from someone or something as quickly as possible.

I turned to look in the back seat at the children and my heart sank. I had seen those expressions before – fear, uncertainty, desperation and longing. So much for young lives to take in and make sense of when everything going on was senseless. Then a strange thing occurred. I watched as a round clear tube exited

Malcolm's chest and began floating backward over the seat toward the children. As it neared them, it split into two smaller tubes, entering the respective chests of the children near where their hearts were located. I got the distinct impression that this was some sort of emotional umbilical cord. Then it hit me! All the emotions – the anxiety, the panic, the desperation, the paralyzing fear – that controlled Malcolm's actions flowed directly into the children.

Without any of them making a sound, I heard the substance of recent conversations exchanged among them.

"Daddy, what are we going to do? How will we make it without Mommy?"

Malcolm did the best he knew by responding, "We'll get over this someday! We'll forget about the pain. We just WILL! You'll see!"

However, he knew what he was saying was not true and so did the children; yet, they worked as hard as they knew how to pretend that everything would be just like Malcolm said.

In the blink of an eye, I found myself standing next to Angela once again and I knew the reason she wanted me to see her family. "Angela, how can I possibly help you – help *them*?"

For the first time since she stopped me, Angela spoke in soft melodic tones. "You must keep on running and telling fathers that their children need them to be fathers. Tell them that they need to stop speeding through life hoping to outrun the pain. Help them understand that they must embrace the pain of loss as well as the uncertainty of the future."

The Journey

She looked deeply into my eyes and continued. "You must tell them about the importance of creating personal stability so that they can guide their children to live stably as *they* grow. You must tell them to slow down, to feel, to pay attention to their struggles so that they can pay attention to those of their children as well. You must teach them to take side roads and exits to the scenic routes in life. Teach them to slow down and live. Life on this side is ever so brief. Please teach them to live as fully and completely as possible. Please!"

Once again, I felt small and incapable; yet I could not resist her sincerity. "I will do all that I can, Angela, I promise."

As if she sensed my doubt, she said, "You must learn to doubt your doubts and trust your inner strength to guide your steps."

I nodded and turned once again to look out at the Interstate. "Doubt my doubts, huh?"

Another gust of wind whipped dust in my face and I turned to deflect the assault. Angela was gone.

I stood for a moment reflecting on what had happened then instinctively started out once again toward the mountains. The air was growing warmer and I stopped under the shade of an overpass. Placing my hands on my knees, I bent over to catch my breath, closed my eyes and rested briefly.

A sudden blast of cooler air followed by a distant rumble wrested me from my brief respite. To my surprise, I found myself surrounded by darkness. The only light available came from distant lightening. The intermittent flashes revealed snapshot-like glimpses of a location that was familiar. Red dirt, scrubby mesquite trees dotting rugged terrain and rock-filled yet empty stream beds that could be filled with roaring water should a sudden downpour occur. *I knew this place! I was in the Palo Duro Canyon!*

The Journey

~~~~~~~

Growing up in the Panhandle of Texas, I was used to rapidly developing thunderstorms sweeping the plains, so the onslaught of flashing light followed by rumbling peels of thunder were completely familiar. Visiting the Palo Duro Canyon as a child had always been an extremely enjoyable experience! The rugged vistas proved fertile ground for a young boy's imagination and I reveled in the memories that flooded my mind as I stood there enjoying the raw power of nature. In recent years as an adult, I had participated in trail run events to raise funds for the **Journey of Hope** in all kinds of weather – extremes of cold and heat; chilling rain; snow; even a couple of thunderstorms. A brilliant flash of lightening followed immediately by ground-shaking thunder revealed a trail in front of me. I instinctively began traversing the path on which I found myself as if drawn forward by an invisible beacon.

The terrain proved as precarious as I remembered from recent runs through the Canyon. Although I knew that I must continue running, I longed for the assistance of a flashlight – anything to reveal what lay ahead of me. Stumble-sliding over the trail, uncertainty gripped my heart like a vise. Paralyzing fear filled my veins threatening cessation of movement. Without warning, deafening thunder and blinding light simultaneously erupted just over the hill in front of me. So violent was the blast that the ground literally shook beneath my feet causing me to freeze in my tracks. I had *never* experienced lightening or thunder like *that*! What happened next was well . . . nearly indescribable!

The Journey

A tsunami-like surge of invisible force rushed over the hill and struck me square in the chest causing me to stagger backward. Before I could regain my balance, the force field reversed, re-entered from my back and threw me to the ground. I pushed myself to my knees and felt of my chest, convinced that my heart had torn free from my body. I breathed a sigh of relief to discover that I was in one piece. The storm in which I found myself was stranger than any I had ever experienced. I was terrified!

Before I could stand again, I heard a voice off to my right. "Hey, buddy! Over here!"

I looked in the direction of the voice and spied a shadowy figure crouched under a rock overhang. He had a small flashlight and I rapidly crawled toward safety beneath the ledge. As I scooted next to my new companion, I discovered that he was clothed in an Army uniform – complete with helmet, rifle and gear. Then it hit me! *War!* Not a thunderstorm!

Charles was his name – he was a Captain in the Army. The blast that shook me only moments ago had actually removed Charles from the battle – permanently – and thrust him into the "Place of Passage" without warning. When I looked into his eyes, I knew that *he* knew as well and needed no further explanation.

Charles reached into his pocket and retrieved a photograph. The glow of the flashlight revealed four smiling faces – that of Charles, his wife Anna and their two lovely daughters – a moment frozen in time when all was well with their world. I reached for the picture to get a closer look. The moment my fingers touched the paper, a sense of regret and despair gripped my heart. I looked into Charles' eyes. Anna and the girls had found out that he would not be coming home again – at least not in the manner in which he had promised. I choked back tears – tears for *them*; tears for all the other families of soldiers who had received similar news or would in the days to come.

The picture suddenly became a small viewing screen – a screen on which I witnessed the devastation and heartbreak that engulfed Anna and the girls when authorities delivered the news. The physical, emotional, mental, spiritual and relational pain inflicted by that single explosion half-way around the world, shook that family to the very core of its foundation. They would need comfort, guidance and protection – all gifts that Charles desperately wished to give. They would require love, understanding and support – all necessities that others would need to provide. Their road to reconciliation would be as tough and treacherous of the one on which I traveled – even more so!

Charles took back the photograph and the vision dimmed. As the scene faded, I remember seeing family and friends gathering around Anna and the girls and I felt heartened. I looked at him and started to speak, but was only able to say, "What . . ." before sobs choked the rest of my question.

Charles spoke in a deep baritone voice that immediately soothed my frayed emotions. "You are already on the road, my friend, doing what must be done. Please continue to tell our story and the stories of countless others like us! For it is only in telling the stories that families will find help; that awareness will come; that support arrives. It is only in telling the stories that *my* family will find peace. I am depending on you to carry out this mission."

"But I am only one," I recall saying, feeling completely overwhelmed.

"The journey of a million miles is taken one step at a time," he responded. "Others will join you – in fact they are as we speak. You are not alone in this quest! Persevere, my friend. Persevere!"

I was exhausted! I closed my eyes for what seemed only a moment, but much more time passed. I awoke to the sound of a hawk soaring overhead. When I opened my eyes, Charles was gone and the sky bore the telltale signs that daybreak approached. I stood, stretched and made my way back to the trail. Feeling a bit revived, I commenced my run up hill. At the exact moment I reached the top, the sun broke above the horizon sending a blinding ray of light into my eyes. I raised my hand as a shield and ducked my head. Coming to a stop to regain vision, I looked up to find myself on the barren, windswept plains outside a city off in the distance.

The Journey

Once again, that internal guidance system prodded me to run – to move toward the city limits ahead of me. This time, there was no path, no trail to follow. I simply ran in the direction my heart commanded. Eventually, I found myself on the outskirts of Lubbock, TX, – a city in which I had lived when I was a young boy. A grove of trees surrounded by metal fencing beckoned me forward. I was not completely surprised to find myself at the gate of a small cemetery.

After standing at the gate for a moment, I entered and began walking through the memorials inscribed with emotion-laden words for loved ones interred there. Rounding the expanse of a rather large cedar tree, I came upon a young boy sitting on a bench in the middle of the memorial park. As I approached, he stood and turned to face me as if he expected me. A big smile spread across his face as he saw me walking toward him. A surge of emotion welled in me. Tears began flowing down my cheeks. I knew this little boy! He was familiar to me but that was impossible! How could I know someone I had never met?

When we were but twenty or so feet apart, he broke and ran toward me with his arms wide open. Instinctively, I knelt to receive his embrace. He crashed into me and we tumbled backward to the ground. He held tightly to my neck and I heard him say, "I am so glad you are here! I am so glad! I have waited so long for this!"

I was confused! He let go and we got up off the ground. I continued to kneel in front of the little guy and held him at arms-

The Journey

length to determine how I knew him. He certainly seemed to know me!

As I looked at him, it was almost as if I were staring at myself at about age three. Although there were distinct similarities, he was definitely not *me*! I studied and studied his features and then the dawn broke. *He* knew the moment recognition occurred and flashed a big, toothy grin. "Sydney!" I remember saying in disbelief.

He threw his arms around my neck once again and I began to weep. Sydney – my brother who never was! The blessed addition to our family back in 1956, never added. The one about whom our family rarely spoke after the day he was stillborn. All my life, I had wondered about Sydney – about what it would have been like to have a younger brother. In the years following that family tragedy, I recalled playing "make believe" – creating games and circumstances where Sydney and I would play together. I couldn't believe my eyes!

I picked him up and we sat together on the bench and just looked at one another for a long time. Finally, Sydney reached for my hand. As his tiny hand encircled my thumb, I found myself taken back to the small house in which we lived back then. Although the memories were fuzzy, I was able to recall the confusion that I experienced. Our home was to have been happy when mommy came home from the hospital. We were supposed to have a little "bundle of joy!" They had said so! Instead, there were tears; hushed conversations filled with emotions I couldn't comprehend; buried anger and resentment; blame; sadness; and the sense of barrenness created by an empty cradle.

The experience of adulthood had given meaning to all those conflicting and confusing feelings from the past. Looking back, I can see how that event initiated life-long reverberations of grief for all of my family – parents, grandparents, aunts and uncles. So much possibility unfulfilled. So many hopes dashed. So many dreams erased. So much happiness buried. More than 60 years have passed and I still feel the sting of that day.

I closed my eyes allowing the scene to disappear, and then looked down again into Sydney's face. "I don't understand little bro! What does *this* have to do with *my* journey? Why are we here together *now* of all times?"

Sydney looked up at me and with wisdom well beyond his years, he said, "Your journey began on that day – the journey you continue even now. What was incomprehensible then you now have words to describe. With those words, you can comfort young mothers and fathers – help mend hearts and relationships torn apart by the unthinkable. You can teach others to express compassion for families tormented by the emptiness of early death. You can help create hope for the future. You can do this because healing matters!"

Sitting there on that bench, I thought about all the challenges that Sydney's absence from our lives had created for my family through the years. I thought about the impact of his absence in my own life. How many times growing up had I heard, "Do you have a brother?" He was right! My journey *had* begun the day *his* terminated. I have been running this race for a very long time. I realized that to drop the running now would mean taking my eye off the finish line – stopping short of the goal – missing chances to make a difference.

Sydney squeezed my hand bringing me back to that special moment. As I looked at him again, I knew that my time to depart had come. I didn't want to leave! I had so many things to ask him – so many things to tell him. Looking into his eyes however, I realized that telling him wasn't necessary. He already knew. He had been with me more times throughout my life than I was aware. I gave him a big hug and sat him back on the bench.

"See ya, Big Bro!" He shouted out as I began the next leg of my journey.

"See ya, Syd!" I yelled back as tears welled in my eyes making it difficult to see. I stopped one last time to wave to him. As we waved, he simply dematerialized before my eyes, disappearing from sight . . . but not from my heart.

I continued to run east completely lost in thought and unaware of what was building behind me. When the air suddenly carried a hint of fine mist that smelled of dirt, I knew what was coming. I turned to see a great wall of red roiling toward me, perhaps fifty feet high. It was on me before I could react. I simply rolled into a ball covering my eyes, nose and mouth and waited. The sand storm swept over me like a giant wave in the ocean. The stinging sand peppered my skin leaving me feeling as if a million mosquitoes had attacked at once.

The onslaught was over as quickly as it began. As the wind died down, I opened my eyes to discover yet another locale – the

The Journey

path on which I started this strange journey. I found myself approaching the mega stadium that stretched far into the heavens filled with people cheering words of encouragement. Perhaps my journey had ended and I could return home. Perhaps I could . . .

From behind me, I heard the voice of a woman. "Girl on your left!"

I stopped and moved to the side a step or two. Riding up behind me was a woman with a million-dollar smile. She was so radiant that her countenance literally glowed. She rolled to a stop in front of me and took off her helmet.

"Beverly! What . . .?"

"Pretty cool, isn't it? I had no idea! No idea whatsoever!"

I needed no explanation or introduction. Beverly was one of the most inspirational people I knew. She was a trooper in every sense of the word! Her life was a living testimonial to the power of hope; the power of belief; the power of healing! To so many she will always be THE beacon in the darkness!

She looked at me and said, "We are similar, you and I. We share the same passion for helping people – the same dedication to make a difference. That's why I ran and biked and swam – to make a difference; to help others experience the hope in healing." After the death of her husband, Beverly participated in triathlons to raise awareness and funds for the **Journey of Hope**. She and her children had experienced such wonderful support in the aftermath of their personal tragedy. Participating in the athletic events was her way of giving back to **The Journey**!

"Beverly, you are such an inspiration and so very missed by everyone – especially your family!" I said.

"I really left too soon – much sooner than I had intended. I left so much undone! I want so much for them all to heal – to grow in hope and personal peace."

Then she looked at me and said, "It will take you and many others like you to carry on the race – to help my family – to tell others about the power of hope and healing. Please continue, no matter what! Please!"

No way could I resist that request! "Of course, Beverly. Of course I will!"

She smiled at me with that classic smile, donned her helmet once again and rode on ahead. I could hear the roar of the crowd increase several decibels as she pumped through the finish line! It was amazing!

"Now what?" I remember saying to myself. "Now what?"

~~~~~~~

No sooner had the words escaped my lips than I found myself back at the beginning place – still, quiet, peaceful. Light from an unknown source above filtered down casting a clearly defined shadow on the floor. As I looked down, the shadow detached from my feet and once again, Coach was standing in front of me.

"You OK?"

I looked back into those strange, explosively powerful eyes and simply nodded. He reached out and patted me on the shoulder squeezing it affectionately as he did so. My head was spinning; my heart racing; my emotions spent.

"I thought you said you'd see me down the road! Where'd you go, man?"

"Oh, I was with you the entire way – step-for-step," he responded.

"But I didn't see you, how . . ."

He interrupted, "Seeing me or not has nothing to do with my real presence with you the whole trip. I was there – and always will be."

"I guess it's time for me to get back to . . . well, where I came from?" I asked half-way hoping that he would say no.

"Yes. It is time. I just want to make sure that you have the answers you seek. Do you?" He asked.

I think he knew the answer even before he asked. Of course I did! I had more than enough answers.

He just smiled and looked upward. As he did, a transparent

oblong circle opened above me revealing the full moon once again. A breeze from above caused the transparent surface to ripple and I realized that I was looking up *through* my puddle.

Dumbfounded, I started to speak once again to Coach, but he stopped me. Instead, he said, **"*Run with endurance the race that is set before you*!"**

As quickly as I had fallen into that strange underworld, I found myself on the surface once again foot planted firmly in the middle of the puddle and chilled water droplets peppering my legs! "What in the world . . . ?"

I stopped so quickly that I almost slid down. I walked back over to the puddle and timidly touched my toe to the surface and pushed down. Yep! Solid concrete! I wondered if I was losing it. Not sure what to make of what had just occurred; I terminated my morning run and turned back toward the house, walking slowly, working to make sense of my jaunt into the Twilight Zone.

Back home, I sat for a long time in the silence of my study, unsure of what to believe. I was just about to chalk the whole experience to a vivid imagination, when I became aware of my right hand balled into a tight fist – so tight that it threatened to cramp. I pried each finger open individually and to my surprise, discovered a small oblong, slightly teardrop shaped silver disc – the same disc that Coach had placed there prior to my journey. I turned it over and discovered a spiral similar to what a coiled snake might look like – tightly curled in the center extending outward. Instinctively, I knew its meaning – the continuity of life; the expansion of spiritual understanding; growth and power.

It *had* happened after all. It was no dream! I decided, then-and-there, to avoid questioning the reality of that experience! I determined to act upon the lessons learned. I took that special disc, placed it on a leather cord and wear it every day to remind myself that I have a race set before me that I must complete.

I am unable to say that the Journey is easy. It is not! Sometimes, I feel as if it is too much – that the burdens and challenges far outweigh my capacities. I often feel alone and misunderstood. In those moments of self-doubt, I direct my mind to focus on the strange encounters I had in that **Place of Passage**. I reflect on the realities of living that were secured in my spirit and as a result and my resolve returns. I feel encouraged and Hopeful once again! I am convinced that I CAN take that next step and the next and the next and . . .

The journey of a million miles is taken one step at a time. It will take all of us to make a difference! Won't you join me on this journey?

Peace!

Works Cited

McEwan, Steve & Wiseman, Craig, Writers: ***That's What It's All About***, BMI/ASCAP. Performed by Brooks and Dunn: "The Greatest Hits Collection II" 2004. Arista Records & BMG Music, Nashville, TN.

Holy Bible, Hebrews 12:1-3, 12, adapted and paraphrased from the New International Version, Zondervan Publishers, Grand Rapids, MI.

Acknowledgements

I am grateful to my wife Vanessa for her undying faith in me and what I work at doing! Without her love and support my thoughts and ideas might still be swimming around in my head.

I am grateful to my children and grandchildren who are a constant source of joy and amazement! When I spend time with them, they inspire me to be a better person!

I am grateful for all my friends who continually offer support, encouragement and guidance as I work to figure out what I want to do when I grow up! Thanks for weathering my multiple "Bald Moments" dear friends!

Peace!

About the Author

Mark E. Hundley is a bald headed Texas Cowboy Therapist who loves to connect with people from all walks of life! He is the author of **Awaken to Good Mourning** and **Ten Surefire Strategies to Live a Better Life** – books written to help people embrace the challenges inherent in life and create meaning in the process! Both books are available on Kindle. He has also published works of short fiction on Kindle under "The Place of Passage" series.

Throughout his professional career, Mark has discovered power in the telling of a good story. In fact, he shares that some of the most profound truths he has ever learned have come as the result of a simple story. He uses stories in everything he does – writing, speaking, teaching and counseling.

Mark lives in Texas with his wife Vanessa. They have three grown children together (a "family on the blend") and three grandsons. He received his BA in Sociology from Hardin-Simmons University in Abilene, TX, and his masters in Counseling from the University of North Texas in Denton, TX.

markhundley32@gmail.com

"The one who tells the stories rules the world." Hopi Proverb

Made in the USA
Columbia, SC
07 March 2025